Ted,
Thank you for being you!
Always remember how much you are Loved!
Suzanne

All Children are Gifted:
Raising Confident and Aware Children

All Children are Gifted:
Raising Confident and Aware Children

SUZANNE CARTER

Copyright © 2016 Suzanne Carter, M.A.

All rights reserved. No part of this book may be used or reproduced by any means, graphic, electronic, or mechanical, including photocopying, recording, taping or by any information storage retrieval system without the written permission of the author except in the case of brief quotations embodied in critical articles and reviews.

Archway Publishing books may be ordered through booksellers or by contacting:

Archway Publishing
1663 Liberty Drive
Bloomington, IN 47403
www.archwaypublishing.com
1 (888) 242-5904

Because of the dynamic nature of the Internet, any web addresses or links contained in this book may have changed since publication and may no longer be valid. The views expressed in this work are solely those of the author and do not necessarily reflect the views of the publisher, and the publisher hereby disclaims any responsibility for them.

Any people depicted in stock imagery provided by Thinkstock are models, and such images are being used for illustrative purposes only.
Certain stock imagery © Thinkstock.

ISBN: 978-1-4808-3267-1 (sc)
ISBN: 978-1-4808-3268-8 (e)

Library of Congress Control Number: 2016909436

Print information available on the last page.

Archway Publishing rev. date: 7/11/2016

Dedicated to my son,

Christopher James Addison Cross Carter
On August of 1988 at the Miracle Mountain Retreat, when
Alan Cohen asked: "What would you do if nothing
were standing in your way", and
my answer came clearly to me like a shooting star across a velvet black sky:
HAVE CHRISTOPHER..........My life suddenly took on its true meaning.
Christopher, being your mother has been and will always be the greatest joy
of my life. However, having the privilege of being your mother has enabled
and empowered me to be more of who I am. My greatest hope is that being
your mother has empowered you to be more of the "Wondrous Child of
God", (from the Daily Word on the day that you were born) that you are.
When I think of you, I am filled with great joy and deep gratitude.
Thank you Christopher for letting me be your mother.
You are such a gifted person in so many ways and now as
your career of being an amazingly gifted musician takes
off, I am so proud of you, my soul sings with JOY.
Thank you too for doing the first edit; the book
would not have happened without you.

And to my mom, Bea Drake: Your willingness to listen to your own Inner
Knowing that led you to new lands at such a young age-- joining the
Army at the age of 18, and to owning your own business at the age of 24.
You have empowered me deeply and in all ways. Your pioneer spirit, love
of adventure, fun, and laughter live in my blood, my bones, my heart,
Mom. Plus, you get the award for the best Mamau in the Universe.

Please find a list of people I thank from the bottom of my heart at
the end of the book plus a list of acknowledgements of other people
who may add sustenance to your own authentic journey.

Contents

About the Author ix
Introduction xi
Summary of Chapters xiii

Chapter 1   Inner Knowing 1
Chapter 2   Listening to Others and Self 8
Chapter 3   Safety 16
Chapter 4   Dreams 20
Chapter 5   Teaching Right and Wrong 24
Chapter 6   Are You Listening Too? 30
Chapter 7   Discipline from the Heart 33
Chapter 8   Healing a Good World 37
Chapter 9   Trust: The Gift of Teaching Yourself and Your Child to Listen to Their Inner Knowing 42

More Acknowledgements 49

About the Author

Suzanne Carter is an ordained minister and an eclectic therapist drawing upon many schools of thought, enabling individuals who attend her workshops to get in touch with and manifest their truest selves. She offers a unique approach by blending psychology, spirituality, and mind-body health principles. The workshop participants are encouraged to address all of their issues in a safe and supportive way. Her commitment is to facilitate wholeness in all levels of one's being: spiritual, psychological, physical, intellectual, and social. Suzanne has worked as a co-minister with her husband for the last thirty years, serving Unity Churches in Missouri, Washington, Michigan, and Colorado.

Suzanne has presented workshops for the last thirty years and is an excellent speaker and workshop facilitator. Topics she has presented include codependency, women's issues, death and dying, couples' issues, and attaining optimum health through nutrition, exercise, and stress management. Suzanne believes that wholeness or total wellness can only be attained by treating the individual on a holistic level.

The importance of getting in touch with the erroneous thoughts and beliefs that are programmed into individuals at a very early age is central to Suzanne's work.

These damaging thoughts and beliefs are often the crux of the myriad of problems that people experience. For example, when people have a belief that they are not good enough, this belief will usually manifest as physical, psychological, or spiritual problems. Suzanne's approach helps individuals get in touch with these negative beliefs, feel their feelings, and then release them to make room for a more realistic and truthful view of who they are. Suzanne believes that all humans are basically good, but if they have been taught otherwise, their thoughts, words, actions, and beliefs will be in accordance with what they have learned.

Suzanne holds a Bachelor's degree in Psychology from the University of Indiana and a Master's degree in psychology from the University of Colorado Denver (1981) and was graduated and ordained by the Unity School of Religious Studies in 1986. She has received extensive training in psychodrama and experiential therapy through Onsite Training and Consulting, Inc., in Tucson, Arizona. She is certified with the Grief Recovery Institute in California and is a certified equine-assisted psychotherapist with EAGALA. She is also a Spiritual Intelligence coach with Deepchange.com. She is in private practice in the greater Denver area.

Suzanne truly travels the path that she presents. She has a multifaceted health program in which she engages on a daily basis. She is in excellent health and believes that it is every human's birthright to be whole, well, and free and able to achieve happiness in every area of life. Suzanne lives in Morrison, Colorado, with her husband and her animal co-therapists, Jessie, the golden prince and Harmony, an equine princess. Her son lives in Fort Collins and is a musician par excellence.

She has presented workshops in her hometown of Denver as well as in Kansas City, Missouri; Grand Rapids, Michigan; Indianapolis, Indiana; and Seattle, Washington.

Introduction

If you look around at the seemingly endless problems in the world and want to do something to solve them, this book can help you. It has been especially written for parents, soon-to-be parents, teachers, and caregivers who look into the eyes of a child and see that the little girl or boy is filled with infinite possibilities of good. I believe that as we help our children, we are helping heal our world, one emotionally healthy child at a time

We will solve the problems of the world only when we become aware of our innate goodness, connect with this inner wisdom that is part and parcel of this goodness, and then express that goodness in our lives every day. If you believe in the inherent goodness of all people and you are willing to focus on and magnify that goodness, you *can* change the world. When you help a child understand the Truth of his or her goodness, you are not only doing something wonderful for the child, but you are also helping to heal the world.

These two spiritual truths—humanity and all of creation are innately good; and the resources of this goodness are directly available to each person—are the guiding principles in this book. I've chosen to call this innate wisdom and goodness that is to each always available of us the "inner knowing."

I have presented the information in language that can be understood by everyone, regardless of religious background and present beliefs. Reading this book will not make parenting hassle-free or even easier. Rather, when applied to daily life, these ideas will make parenting more challenging because you will see children as individuals who should have the opportunity to express ideas about their lives and be guided about making age appropriate choices.

However, these ideas provide a firm foundation for parenting and raising healthy children to become whole adults. As you nurture children in this manner, you will know that you are doing the best job possible, and that you have been responsible for helping a child fulfill his or her role in solving the problems of the world. You will empower these children to make their dreams come true.

As you read, I trust you will listen to your own inner knowing voice just as you recognize it in your child.

Bless you on your journey. You are loved.

Suzanne Carter

Summary of Chapters

Chapter 1: The Inner Knowing

>Readers are introduced to the concept that children and adults are innately good within themselves. Knowledge of the good and how to access that place in oneself is presented as the key to raising emotionally healthy children. The idea of the inner knowing is central to the theories in the book, and it becomes the vehicle for accessing the inner goodness that is within all of humanity.

Chapter 2: Listening to Others and Self

>Active listening skills and the validation of feelings are taught through description and example. These two abilities are integral in helping the child understand the goodness in his own nature and his inner knowing.

Chapter 3: Safety

>The greatest worry of parents is the safety of their children. If children grow up with the awareness that they are good and worthy, they will want to keep themselves safe. If parents teach children to listen to this voice of goodness, children will always know how to keep themselves safe.
>
>This chapter will illustrate two main points. First, if children know they are good, it will be foreign to their consciousness to do something that will cause harm to themselves, for example, using drugs or engaging

in dangerous actions. Second, the inner knowing will always guide us (child, teen, or adult) to actions that will lead to our highest good. If children listen to their inner knowing, they will always be safe, and this awareness puts many parents at ease regarding their children's safety.

Chapter 4: Needs, Problems, and Dreams

As a minister, I have met countless numbers of people who don't know what to do with their lives. They talk about an inner confusion that has been with them through their entire working lives. They aren't sure what to do about their jobs or their marriages. They don't know where to live, how to solve problems, who to be friends with, and so on and so forth. When problems arise, they don't have a clue about how to solve them, and they have abandoned their dreams as if they were million-dollar wishes.

When children are in touch with their inner knowing, they will be aware of their needs, their problems, and their dreams. They will know how to face and solve their problems and make their dreams come true.

Chapter 5: Teaching Right and Wrong

One of the fundamental responsibilities of parents is to teach their children the difference between right and wrong. When parents validate the inner knowing while explaining what is right and wrong, children quickly learn that as they do the right thing, they feel an inner sense of goodness. They also learn that when they intentionally do what they know is wrong, they don't feel "right" inside. As parents validate the inner knowing, children get a sense of what it is like to feel good, and they are motivated to seek this inner integrity.

Chapter 6: Are You Listening, Too?

This chapter will discuss the importance of the parents' willingness to listen to their own inner knowing. As I have been teaching my son about his inner knowing, I have had a remarkable emotional healing. I have become aware at a very deep level that I am also good and I have this inner knowing as well. Of course, I "knew" this in my head before I could ever teach it to my son, and yet, this truth was not ingrained in the fabric of my being. As I have taught this truth and validated the inner knowing in my son, I have experienced it for myself.

Chapter 7: Effective Discipline

One of the hardest decisions parents make is how to discipline their children. The question always arises as to whether a parent should hit his or her child. If parents believe in the innate goodness of their children, they could never hit them. When children are struck by one who supposedly loves them, they not only get the message that they are bad but also that the parent is bad. It is impossible for children to feel truly happy if they believe both they and their parents are bad.

Chapter 8: Healing the World

With all that goes on in the world, it is quite easy for children to develop an attitude that the world is a terrible, scary place to live—particularly if children believe they are bad. On the other hand, if they believe they are good, this view is projected out into the world, and it becomes a self-fulfilling prophecy.

Chapter 9: Trust: The Gift of Teaching Yourself and Your Child to Listen to Their Inner Knowing. This chapter is titled "Trust" because a major gift that comes from listening to one's inner knowing is that we learn to trust ourselves. The only way to trust in any relationship is to first trust ourselves in such a way that we will never betray ourselves in thought, word, or deed.

Chapter 1

Inner Knowing

My son was three years old when we visited my mother in Denver. I decided to drive to the shopping mall and asked him if he wanted to go with me. He said no, but as I got ready to leave, he changed his mind.

"Okay, but you'll have to put on your shoes," I said.

Suddenly, he changed his mind again, and again I headed for the garage. Just as I was getting into the car, he reappeared, ready to join me. "Okay, but this is your last chance to change your mind," I said, feeling rather frustrated. "Get your shoes."

He didn't return. When I found him again, he said, "I changed my mind, Mommy."

Five minutes later, on my way to the mall, I knew he needed me at that moment. I returned to the house, and as I opened the door, I nearly pulled him outside because he was holding the door handle, crying. "Mommy, Mommy, how did you know I wanted to go with you?"

I told him what I know to be the truth. "I just knew because I listened to my inner knowing."

Inner knowing is a type of knowing we all have inside. Some may call this inner knowing their gut instinct or their intuition. Some may call it their conscience. Inner knowing would keep our children safe and protected if we would choose to teach them to listen to it rather than ignore this deep level of authentic knowing. Instead, we tell them to listen to everything outside of themselves.

As we rode to the mall together, I knew I had made a good impression on him. I'd acknowledged the presence of the inner knowing and through my actions, demonstrated the importance of paying attention to it. I took advantage of an opportunity to teach, and he learned an important lesson. I know I could have taught another lesson as well by letting him know of natural consequences. The lesson would be that sometimes we wait too long to decide what we want. I used natural consequences all the time, but in this instance, my inner knowing told me to return.

I believe the most important thing we can teach children is that they are innately good. That is, who they are is good, and we as parents and caregivers teach them of their goodness first and foremost by how we treat them. There are many ways to wrap our understanding around this innate goodness. Some may think about this essential goodness as a reflection of the divine. Others may simply know that we are born into "original goodness" and not into what some religions call "original sin." Another way to understand that our children and all creatures—whether of fur, fin, feather, or skin—are innately good is to simply look into the faces of our children or out into nature and breathe into our own inner knowing. The fact of innate goodness will flow from our deepest understanding if we choose to look.

Humans have a sense of right and wrong that we can utilize and tap into. Whether we call it intuition, a gut feeling, a hunch, God, or a small voice, as we learn to listen to it, we discover at a very deep level that we are in fact innately good. The presence of good within us eliminates the damaging idea that we're innately bad, despite what traditional religion has hammered into us over the years. We must be willing to know this truth about our natural goodness and take advantage of every opportunity to help our children experience it too. This is the premise of this book: to know of our own goodness and to teach our children this profound truth now. I believe the healing of our world depends on it.

Many children grow up thinking they are bad. They believe there is something profoundly wrong with them. This belief causes them to put on masks—sometimes many masks—to hide something they have been taught to be ashamed of.

Before my son was born, I began praying for a method I could use to teach my son about his innate goodness. The concept of inner knowing was born in my consciousness. I wanted to teach my child about his goodness. I wanted my child to grow from the inside out and to know that his needs, feelings, thoughts, and perceptions were good.

Children learn to look to the outer world for validation and approval. If they aren't taught to be connected to this sense of inner goodness and to listen to this inner knowing, they lose their connection to their inner knowing. Thus, a child's sense of his or her goodness will be determined by how others treat the child. To the degree they believe they're bad, they either behave badly or try to prove they are good, according to the world's standard of outer success and achievement. To the degree they are taught that *who* they are is good even when their behavior needs correction, their behaviors will reflect this inner belief.

Many of our children grow into adulthood having drowned out their inner knowing. They don't have a clue about their true nature being good. Then, as adults, they teach their children the same untruth, and the myth that there is something fundamentally wrong with us gets perpetuated from one generation to the next.

As I mentioned earlier, we are all born into original virtue and goodness, not original sin. At some level, children know this truth. When you validate this knowledge, you give the child the greatest gift of all—the gift of the self. The child learns the true self is good. With that knowledge, the child can reach his or her full potential.

That means parenting will be effortless and free of challenges, right? The opposite may be more accurate. As parents validate the self in the child, the child will be more inner-directed and realize he or she is worthy of making choices about life. It's important to be a strong parent and able to provide structure, loving guidance, and a home environment that is democratic in the truest sense of the word. I'm not suggesting the child should have the last word, but the process of making decisions about the child's life must include his or her thoughts and feelings.

As the child grows, give him or her more opportunities to make choices, always teaching the importance of listening to the inner knowing. It is easy to teach children this because they naturally understand. All you need do is to validate in language that they can understand. It's a process of reminding them of the truth.

One of the easiest ways to teach children about their inner knowing is to validate their ideas. Their ideas come from within themselves, and if you can acknowledge this as a parent, you are telling them what comes from inside them is good. For example, my son was quite verbal. I found ways to consult him about his daily routine. As much as possible, I gave him choices about what he would wear, eat, and do. When challenges arose, I often asked him what he thought would be a good next step. He always had a thought, and I reminded him that his ideas come from within himself. When he would show me some of his artwork, I told him that the ideas behind the work really enabled him to make a beautiful creation. Whenever he came up with a spontaneous idea, I tried as much as possible to validate it, reminding him of where it came from, even if it was not something we would act on.

Validating the child's way of expressing himself or herself, especially during the critical formative years from birth to age two, helps the child develop a relationship to the inner knowing. It's very important to let the child know that every feeling is okay. One does this by naming or labeling the feeling that the child is expressing. When the baby is crying and you know he or she is hungry, you say, "You are so hungry." When the child is sad, you allow yourself to be present to the child's sadness by saying, "You are feeling so sad right now."

It is amazing how well this simple technique works to help a child move beyond sadness or other "negative" emotions.

I put *negative* in quotes because the emotion is simply an emotion, neither positive nor negative. But as a society, we have learned to call sadness, fear, and anger "negative emotions." These emotions are simply ways our emotional bodies help us understand the impact some outer experience is having on us.

It's is equally amazing how infrequently parents allow themselves to be present to their children's negative feelings. In most cases, parents minimize, invalidate, and attempt to fix, or even ridicule their children and their negative feelings. A simple example of this regards sadness. The very experience of being human involves loss, and loss innately stimulates a feeling of sadness. The most effective statement a parent could say to a child when a son or daughter feels sad about anything is to let the child know the parent knows about the sadness.

One might say, "I can see that you are feeling very sad about this. I understand, and I would be sad too. I'm going to be right here with you as you feel your sadness."

What parents, adults, teachers, caretakers, and the majority of adults do when around children who are crying or expressing sadness is to tell them in one way or another why the child should not feel sad. The adult often intellectualizes the incident that stimulated the sadness, and this in no way truly helps the child deal with the sadness.

An example of intellectualizing a loss for a child would be to tell a child, "Tomorrow, we will buy you a new dog to replace the one that died. Don't feel sad.

We will take care of this tomorrow. Death is a part of life, just the way leaves falling off a tree in the fall is part of life."

Some of the things we say after a loss may be true factually, but to simply intellectualize without being present to the feelings is true emotional illiteracy.

This simply tells the child that this adult, whom the child in many cases needs in order to survive, is telling him or her not to feel his or her feelings. So, year after year, as this happens, the child eventually becomes a teen who does not have a clue what he or she is feeling and the teen becomes an adult who is out of touch with his or her feelings. Now is it any wonder why grief, which is the natural, healthy, and normal response to any loss, is experienced as something that simply cannot be handled? The truth is we can handle loss if we were taught that all feelings are okay and we have the ability to deal with all of our feelings.

In the same way, invalidating feelings is probably one of most effective ways to teach a child that his or her inner expressions are wrong and thus, bad. Unfortunately, this practice takes place in the majority of all family homes, according to John Bradshaw, well-known author, lecturer, and theorist.

Again, every human feeling is okay. It is okay simply because it is there. We may not have been brought up understanding this; however, validating a child's feelings is one of the greatest gifts we can give our children. Every child needs to be taught that every feeling is okay. At the same time, it is up to us to teach them that every action is not okay. For children under two years of age, validating their expressions and redirecting them is probably the best way to teach them that their inner experiences are good. As the child grows in cognitive abilities, the parent/caregiver must use firmer limits while still being willing to validate the child's experiences and expressions of emotion.

My intention is not to teach basic parenting techniques in this book. There are many good books available on how to deal with each stage of the child's development. I recommend going to a local bookstore and asking where the books on parenting are. Then, take some time and pick out three that seem to resonate with your inner knowing. Then, I suggest reading them before the child is born.

By the age of two, the child is learning to speak and already has developed many comprehension skills. A parent enhances the child's awareness of the inner knowing when the parent calls it by name. For example, when children make a wise choice or come up with a good idea, telling them that they must have been listening to their inner knowing is a simple and effective way to teach them about their inner knowing. When they are learning a new skill and are very frustrated, have them stop and listen to their inner knowing or simply reflect to them what you believe they are feeling. It's remarkable how well this technique works. Listening to themselves is probably the most important skill parents can teach their children.

When our son was learning to ride his bicycle, he would get very frustrated. We would too. Often, we would find ourselves telling him *not* to be frustrated (a feeling) and to just get back on his bike (note how we were invalidating his feeling). What would usually happen is that he would become even more frustrated. However, during the times when we would *remember* to reflect his feelings first, he would often be able to get back on his bike even before we suggested it. Another helpful technique was to gently touch his shoulder, acknowledge his frustration, and ask him to take a couple of deep breaths. When we would remember to do this, he automatically would change his focus from the bike to himself. Almost instantly, he felt better.

One of the deepest pains a person, child, or adult will ever experience is the pain of being disconnected from him or herself and his or her inner knowing. When we are taught to always focus outside of ourselves, it is very easy to disconnect from our inner knowing. It is the parent/caregiver's job to remind the child to connect to her inner knowing. The best way to remind our children is to also stay connected to our own inner knowing, including an awareness of our own feelings.

The reason it is so painful to be disconnected from ourselves is because it is through our *selves* that we truly experience intimacy. True intimacy occurs when one can share all feelings, experiences, perceptions, and thoughts with another person and have them validated and vice versa. For example, when people lose a job, they will automatically have thoughts that they have failed, and they will naturally have feelings of sadness, fear, and anger. When a close friend is willing to be in touch with these same feelings and to validate these feelings in his or her friend who lost the job, the one who lost the job feels understood. When one is understood, one can reconnect to hope and be able to take action based on this hope. Normally what happens, however, is a close friend will say those intellectual truisms like, "Oh, don't worry, you will find another job," "When one door closes, another opens," and on and on and on. These things might be true in some cases, but they almost never help the person who has lost his or her job feel better. It is not the friend's job to make the one who lost the job feel better anyway; a true friend will be willing to simply be with or be present to his or her friend while he or she is in this vulnerable place. When people feel understood and not so alone, they will automatically begin the grieving process. The grieving process brings understanding, and when people understand or can make sense of any loss, they can move forward.

In summary, when we teach our children the value of their inner knowing, we are giving them the gift of connection to themselves first and foremost. From this place of inner connection they will experience confidence, the ability to have true emotional intimacy with another, and self-respect. What greater gifts could we give them?

Chapter 2

Listening to Others and Self

When my son was three years old, he was around someone who liked teasing him, calling him funny names that had nothing to do with him or with what he was doing. He did not like it. He asked the person to stop, and the person agreed to stop based on one condition.

The adult said, "I'll stop calling you this if you are a good boy."

My son replied almost immediately, "I'm always a good boy. Sometimes I do things that aren't good ideas, but I'm always good." The adult was left speechless, and she never called my son a derogatory name again.

About a year and a half later, at age four and a half, my son was having a conversation with his six-year-old friend. The friend told him, "No one was good except Jesus." My son replied that Jesus taught that all of us are good, but sometimes we do things that aren't good. The friend rephrased his belief: "No one is perfect except Jesus."

My son replied, "My mommy thinks I'm perfect."

These two examples illustrate the value of teaching our children that they are inherently good. If a child truly believes he is good, he simply won't buy into negative judgments other people may express. When attacked, children tend to counterattack, wishing to hurt the other person because they feel hurt. When they believe the truth—that they are good—they are able to refrain from counterattack and instead respond from their inner knowing. Without trying they may become the attacker's teacher while keeping themselves safe. Another benefit of teaching our children of their essential goodness is that they often wind up with a wide variety of friends because of this inner confidence that comes naturally as a result of knowing of their innate goodness. My son was friends with people in all groups at school, from the most popular to the groups or children that were not so popular. His teachers would tell me that because of his friendliness to students who were not so popular, they automatically enlarged their circle of friends by simply being with my son.

Certainly, this won't happen all the time with young children or even adolescents, but it will happen some of the time. It is a beautiful thing to behold children learning at a very young age to fight fair and also to love unconditionally. That is, they respond from within themselves, speaking their own truth rather than focusing completely on the outer.

Children are able to do this because they believe they are good and have been taught to listen inwardly to and respond from this belief. They do not have to react or defend a false part of themselves. They are one whole, integrated package of good and can live their lives in this awareness.

When our son had a power struggle with one of his school friends, he almost always wanted to tell me about it. I did my best to take the time to listen whenever he was ready to tell me so I could truly be present to his feelings, and he almost always felt better after he talked with me. Invariably within a few days at the most, he was ready to make up with his friends. Often, he was willing to understand his friend's perspective as well. Even into college, our son was able to be present to other students when they were dealing with loss. Typically, by the time people are young adults, they have learned that when someone is facing a huge loss like the loss of a parent or the breakup of a relationship, there is really nothing one can say, so the person facing the loss is isolated. This is the opposite of what needs to happen, but it nevertheless is what occurs. I saw my son, time and time again, seeking out the one who was dealing with a huge loss, and the main thing he would do was simply be present. This ability to be present occurs when people have been told that *who* they are is good, and then they know that their presence may be all that is necessary.

When we listen to children, they learn to listen. They also learn that what they believe, feel, think, and say is important. If they believe this about themselves, they quite naturally believe it about others. It is a universal truth that what we think about others is a reflection of what we think about ourselves.

One of the easiest ways to teach children to listen to themselves and others is by using active listening. Active listening involves reflecting back to children what you heard them say. In the beginning, when first using this technique, you may need to repeat what they said word for word. If you have a loving tone, however, the child won't believe you're mimicking him. As you develop the skill, you will learn to summarize what they said and begin to reflect back the *feelings* that were present for the child as he or she was talking. This kind of listening validates the child's entire being. That is, it gives the child the sense that you understand or are willing to understand. It tells the child that you are not judging him for what he has done or has felt or how he thinks or believes. You are giving the child the message that you understand him. Finally, and most importantly, it tells the child that you value him enough to listen and converse with him about what he is trying to say.

Active listening is not only effective with children. This kind of listening can greatly benefit all relationships and not just those with children. It certainly brought about peace in a family that was used to only talking at each other. The following is an example of what happened in this family.

The Jones family (fictitious names) had five family members—Mom, Dad, two daughters, and one son. The typical family interaction involved the father ordering and directing the lives of the four other family members. The mother sat passively back, afraid, while the two daughters did their best to comply with their father's orders. The son, the oldest, was a rebel and often got into yelling matches with his father. I was doing family therapy with this family, and the following is a brief excerpt from a session in which the son and father were present. The two of them were asked to use active listening during fifteen minutes of the session and discuss a request that the son had made the week before that had concluded in a huge argument.

Son: Dad, I want to borrow the car on Saturday for the prom. My car isn't running well, and it would be embarrassing to be all dressed up and drive my junker.

Dad: You want to borrow my car because you feel embarrassed about the way your car runs and looks?

Son: That's right. I'm excited about my date, and I'd like to make a good impression. (The week before the son hadn't even gotten this far in telling his father about his feelings of excitement.)

Dad: I'm a little concerned about your taking the car and drinking. (The week before, the father went nearly berserk with accusations that the son would be drinking and he knew the car would be wrecked.)

Son: I can understand your feelings about that. If I can borrow the car, I promise I'll only drink juice and soda. It's really important that I have a nice car. My date, Michelle, is really special. I'd like you to meet her.

Dad: I hear how important this is to you. Let's discuss this with your mother. I think we'll be able to work something out. And I am happy you want to introduce Michelle to us.

This example illustrates how active listening facilitates a natural flow in conversation and encourages the people talking to say more. It is very important to listen to the feelings behind the words. If you can validate a child's feelings by recognizing them and labeling them, your job as a parent can be 100 percent easier. For example, when my son was younger and he came into the house after getting into a power struggle with a friend, he would often show anger by stomping around and even pushing things. My first tendency was to react to his behavior and tell him to knock it off or he'd get a time out or other consequences, etc. When this happens, the child's anger isn't acknowledged, plus the sadness that is often underneath the anger goes completely unrecognized. It gets lost in our interchange, only to be acted out at a later time. If we can restrain our first impulse to stop the immediate behavior, we can then acknowledge the underlying cause of the behavior and truly help solve the problem.

Following are two examples; the first is how not to handle a situation. The second is an example of active listening.

Son comes in, throws backpack down, opens refrigerator, slams it shut, and pushes the dog out of the way. (He had just been told by his best friend that he wasn't invited to his overnighter.)

Mom: "Hey, quit slamming things. And you just hurt the dog! What have I told you about hurting the dog?"

Son stomps out front door, slamming it and grumbling some rude names at his mother.

Active listening:

Son comes in, throws backpack down, opens refrigerator, slams it shut and pushes the dog out of the way. (Same reason as above.)

Mom: "John, you seem really angry."
Son: "You bet I am. I hate that Tim. I never want to see him again.
Mom: "You really feel angry at Tim."
Son: "Yeah, we've been friends for two years, and he's not inviting me to his overnight party."
Mom: "You two have been close for a long time, and you're very disappointed that he's not inviting you to his party."
Son: "Yeah, he's mad at me because I went over to Sam's last week and didn't invite him."
Mom: "Oh, he's feeling hurt and perhaps even jealous?"
Son: "That's right. I'd like to talk about it with him, but when I heard about it all I could see was red."
Mom: "You were so angry initially that you couldn't even talk."
Son: "Yeah, Mom, but I think I can talk to him now. Can I go over there after dinner?"

As we all know, feelings can be all consuming, at least initially, and if they are not acknowledged, named, and validated (valued), they will dictate behavior. That is, if a child is feeling anger and the anger is ignored, the child will act it out. Likewise, if a child is feeling scared and his or her fear is not acknowledged and dealt with, he or she will still be afraid. The child may try to hide it, but it is still there. When a child's fear is continually ignored, the child either has to invalidate him or herself and act macho (unafraid) or will magnify the fear in hopes that someone will acknowledge it. Further, I have seen some children magnify their fears until someone pays attention to them about their fear. The challenge here is that these children learn to get the attention they need by magnifying or exaggerating their fear. Then I have seen these same children become adults who are still walking around "afraid" because they learned that this is the best way to get others to pay attention to their deepest fears.

However, when feelings are validated, they are truly manageable. When my feelings are validated, I feel valuable because feelings are such an intrinsic part of me. When my feelings are ignored, I get a sense that I'm not valued and I feel ignored.

You may be wondering, "If feeling acknowledgment with active listening is so important, then why don't we do it more often?" The answer is that it isn't easy to acknowledge feelings, especially the "negative" ones that have to do with being sad, mad, or scared. We have been taught that these feelings are bad and should be avoided at all costs. Thus, the primary response or reaction to these so-called negative types of feelings is repression and suppression. We have been erroneously led to believe that if we look at negative feelings, we will be engulfed by them and never be free of them. Actually, the opposite is true, and if we are willing to acknowledge them in others and ourselves, they seem to magically disappear. The result is we can think more clearly and *feel* more connected and thus, be our true selves in the world.

Because of our tendency to repress or suppress our feelings, parents can have a very difficult time dealing with their children's feelings. Our society has learned to not value feelings because we feel vulnerable when we are expressing feelings.

So when our child's feelings come up, we have an almost automatic gut level response to "get rid of the feeling." We usually react to the behavior and ignore the feeling. For example, if a child is angry and says, "I hate you," the parent will tend to ignore the feeling of anger and *react* only to the behavior and punish the child. The result is that the child still has the feeling of anger that has now been covered over with a punishment. This does not enable the child to feel good about him or herself or the parent. It serves to make the child feel confused and angry with the parent for the parent's lack of willingness to understand.

Ideally, in a situation like the one described above, the parent would first deal with the feeling of anger by acknowledging it. Then the parent would deal with the child's behavior by letting the child know that although all feelings are okay, we must learn ways to express the feelings but does not attack the other. This simple technique enables children to take responsibility for their feelings and to not blame someone outside of themselves for how they feel.

The inability to express feelings often causes tremendous emotional turmoil and can lead to extreme acting out behavior or severe psychological problems. Many people who work with incarcerated individuals believe that most violent criminals came from severely dysfunctional families where anger and violence were the basis for that family's interactions. However, children from these types of homes are usually not allowed to express their anger. It slowly builds up, and when the child/adult has freedom to express it, it comes out in rage, resentment, and violence. When a child is taught that all feelings are okay and that it is the behavior or the way the feeling is expressed that must be kept in check, this child can grow up emotionally healthy.

As a clinician who sees families, I often spend the first few sessions helping the family create an environment in the home that welcomes feelings. In one family (of course this is a composite story here that brings together the essence of what I am teaching and thus not one family), there were three children and a mom and a dad. The oldest child was going through some really difficult issues at school. Being in a gifted program, he rarely had time for anything but homework, while his younger twin sisters always seemed to have time to play and do whatever they wanted. The oldest child began hitting the twins, and the family came to me when the one of the twins suffered a broken arm when the oldest child pushed her off the porch.

I began by having each member pick a stuffed animal to represent how they were feeling. The oldest child picked a large Tasmanian devil. The other children seemed afraid to pick anything at first, and as I encouraged them, they each picked dogs because "dogs, though nice, are also afraid." The parents were also slow in picking something. It took nearly the entire session to get each family member to do this seemingly simple exercise. The challenge here was that the father actually expressed anger all of the time, the mother was afraid to confront him, and the children were acting out the feelings they saw their parents either expressing, either directly (as the oldest one was doing) or indirectly, as the twins revealed about the mother. I took the opportunity in this session and the next session to talk about how important our feelings are and how very important it is to create an environment where all feelings are okay. In the third and fourth session, we talked about how the oldest child was feeling and what the family needed to do to support him if he was going to remain in such a challenging school program. The twins began to understand how their older brother was feeling and agreed to not tease him anymore in order to get him to pay attention to them. We were able to work out a schedule in which the oldest had more free time not only to play with the twins but also to have some time with friends. The father agreed to go to individual counseling to deal with the anger that stemmed from coming from an abusive family as a child. The mother agreed to work on her own personal power in the family as well. This all began by looking at the feeling environment in the home.

Chapter 3

Safety

My son and I were being seated in a restaurant one day when he was about two years old. The waitress asked if we wanted a table in the smoking section or nonsmoking section. I told her, "Nonsmoking, please, as far away from the smoking section as possible."

When we sat down, my son asked me what smoking was. I explained, "Some people smoke cigarettes, but the smoke makes me cough and I don't like the smell. In fact, eating near the smoke sometimes gives me headaches and spoils the taste of my food."

"But Mommy," my son said, "doesn't it make their food taste funny, too? Doesn't it make them cough and get headaches, too?"

"Yes," I said, "I guess it does."

He gave me a puzzled look. "But why would they do it then, if it makes them feel so bad?"

This is an example of people doing something to their bodies that causes legitimate harm. The research shows that smoking is harmful to one's health and to those around one. I believe that if we can help our children stay connected to their inner knowing from the beginning of their lives, then they will be far less likely to willingly do things to their bodies or even to others that are harmful.

Here is another example of a young child I worked with many years ago. This example, though extreme, demonstrates what can happen more often than we would like to admit when a child is brought up without the understanding of his or her inner knowing and that he or she is inherently good.

The child was a six-year-old girl who was accident-prone. She was not even able to get through one day at school without falling down and hurting herself, sometimes severely enough to require emergency room treatment. On other occasions, a comforting word and a Band-Aid would do the trick. She had no clue about how to keep herself safe. She seemed almost dis-connected from herself and seemed to not understand that she needed to move her body in a certain way to keep from hurting herself. She also seemed to lack the innate sense that she was worthy of being safe.

The little girl didn't seem to possess an inner awareness that she was valuable, and in fact, she seemed almost oblivious to her own pain even when she was clearly hurt.

Again, as I mentioned at the beginning of this chapter, this was a very extreme case, and I use it to illustrate a very important point: to the degree that children are taught they are worthy and valuable is the degree to which they will treat themselves as worthy and valuable. If they are taught by their parents that they must use care when moving their bodies in any given circumstance, they will internalize ways to ensure their safety.

One of the biggest worries of parents is the safety of their children. Many parents are so afraid of the perils and dangers that their children may face that they become overprotective. Many parents believe that the only way to keep their children safe is to watch them constantly. A parent's fear about the dangers children might encounter as they venture out into the world is based on reality and therefore, is valid. However, if you want to raise healthy children with high self-esteem, hovering over them is not the way to accomplish it. In fact, hovering over them and constantly telling them how to be safe will teach them that they can only be safe with the overprotective parent around.

I am talking about two main issues here. First, a child needs to be taught how to move, feel, and get to know the limits and the boundaries of his or her body. Children need to be given experiences that will teach them how to use their bodies in space and time. Physical education is an excellent way for children to learn about their bodies and how they can do a lot of fun things with their bodies.

The second issue is the need to teach children that they are valuable and deserve to be kept safe. The only way parents can truly keep their children safe is to teach them how to keep themselves safe in any situation. The only way to do this is by validating the innate goodness of the child and her inner knowing. When children know they are good, it will be foreign to their inner knowing to do something that will cause harm to themselves, for example, using drugs or engaging in dangerous actions.

The little girl that I spoke of in the beginning of this chapter had two strikes against her with regard to this issue. Not only did she not know how to move her body safely because her parents never had time for her, but she also didn't have a clue about her own worthiness. Following therapy, her accidents became significantly fewer in number. She learned how to move safely, and she also had her inner experiences validated.

On the other end of the spectrum, my son, who has had his inner experience validated and who has been taught to move safely, questions why anyone would intentionally harm him or herself. Further, he has done a great deal of international travel, and although, it is always a bit frightening when he gets on an international flight, I have a deep confidence that he knows his own worthiness, and he also knows how to pay attention to his inner knowing and somehow always knows what to do even when outer circumstances get challenging.

The inner knowing will always guide us—child, teen, or adult—to actions that will lead to our highest good. If children listen to their inner knowing, they will always be safe. This awareness can also put parents at ease when they think about the safety of their children in a dangerous world.

As children grow up listening to their inner knowing, they know at a very deep level when something is not good. When they find themselves in an unpleasant situation, like a poor environment or a bad relationship, they will know what to do. They will calmly leave the situation rather than staying in it and believing that they have to prove their self-worth by valiantly staying to change the situation.

In summary, if children grow into teens and then young adults, learning to treat themselves with love and respect, they will automatically react quite negatively to anyone who is abusive. We often hear about domestic violence cases and how the woman often stays no matter how bad the abuse is. People are baffled by this. As I said above, if people know of their self-worth, when someone treats them badly, they will simply choose to not be around that person any longer. Thus, it is my premise that teaching our children about their own worth by validating their inner knowing will greatly reduce domestic violence.

It is truly amazing how, when even one person knows of the goodness within all people, he or she can transform a seemingly negative situation into a positive one in which problems are solved and harmony is restored.

Chapter 4

Dreams

One beautiful summer evening, my family and I were on a picnic at a sandy beach on Lake Michigan. It was about 6:00 p.m., and we had just finished our meal and had a lot of food left. Our son asked if we could give it to the seagulls that had been coming closer and closer to us as we ate, hoping for a bite we might share with them. We told him yes, and he began throwing bits of crackers and bread out to where they were waiting. As our son continued tossing food, one gull in particular seemed to always get a tasty morsel. In fact, he would come the closest of any of the other gulls and did not seem to be afraid.

My husband decided to see how brave the gull was and held a piece of bread up in the air. The gull, hesitatingly at first, swooped down and grabbed it right out of his hand. We all squealed with delight as my husband continued to hold up morsels of food and this same gull would take the food, fly away to eat it, and then return for more. Other gulls would attempt to fly toward our hands (now all three of us were holding food up, looking like copies of the Statue of Liberty) for the tidbits of food, but none of them would allow themselves to actually take the food except for the one.

This story illustrates to me the magnificence of courage and how inspiring it is when even one individual, be it human or another creature, ventures beyond the typical boundaries of safety, going against the norm, and flies in the face of fear to get what it desires. Now perhaps I am anthropomorphizing here and perhaps this gull did not have any more courage than any of the other gulls. However, this is a great illustration of the courage that comes by connecting with our inner knowing.

We all know of individuals who have done just as this gull did—who have decided to go for it, mustering up enough courage to do all that was necessary to get what they wanted. When we observe a person doing this, we can only stand back and marvel, wondering where they got the courage to truly go for it and succeed.

People who do this must have tremendous courage and confidence in themselves or they could never fly in the face of fear and persevere until success was theirs. Courage means "strength of the heart," and this truly explains how they do what they did—by getting in touch with the strength in their heart. This is another way of talking about listening to the inner knowing.

I discovered this inner courage while I was applying to Unity's ministerial school. I had just received my master's degree, and I had this deep knowing that my next step as far as my career was to go to ministerial school. Though I met all the outer requirements, there was one requirement I did not think I could possibly meet: the requirement of speaking to people on a Sunday morning. In other words, I had no idea how on earth I would ever get over my severe stage fright and be able to give Sunday messages. I almost let this fear keep me from even applying. The one thing that kept me moving forward in the application process was this deep knowing that becoming a Unity minister was something I needed to do. So I proceeded to apply, got through the interview process, and was accepted into school. And though, I did have to wade through a lot of practice talks in which my colleagues wondered if I would ever get over my fear, I can happily say that my inner knowing guided me through school, and I have been speaking on Sunday mornings and in workshop presentations for thirty years.

Another major challenge that arises when people are not connected to their own inner knowing is that they do not know what to do with their lives. They talk, painfully, about an inner confusion that has been with them through their entire working lives. They express thoughts about hating their jobs or even their marriages, and yet they haven't a clue about what to do. Many people have deep frustration about where to live, how to solve problems that plague themselves and their family, with whom to be friends, and so on. The average person doesn't know how to solve problems, and even more devastatingly sad is that they have no idea what they would do in life if they didn't have these problems. They have abandoned their dreams because they were taught from day one to ignore those inner hopes and desires and focus on more practical things.

I believe that the vast majority of all people are not truly in touch with themselves or their deepest dreams. Have you ever asked yourself the question, "What would I do if there were nothing standing in my way?" If you have ever dared to ask this question of yourself; were you able to listen, hear the response, and then take action? I invite you to ask this question of yourself within 24 hours and share with someone you love, what you heard within.

I allowed myself to fall into jobs and even careers in which I was not interested because I didn't have a clue as to who I was, what I was good at, or what I wanted to do. I was other-directed and allowed others' thoughts and perceptions about what would be good for me to sway me in any direction they perceived would be good for me. When I finally began listening within, it was a bit frightening. I began realizing I was not doing what I wanted to, and yet, I didn't know how to *stop* doing what I didn't want to do, let alone find out what I wanted to do. Through my interaction with my clients, workshop attendees, and parishioners at the churches I've served, however, little by little, I began discovering what I wanted to do. Through counseling and attending support group meetings, I not only gained the awareness of what I wanted, but I also gained the confidence to do it.

People who grow up with an awareness of their innate goodness or inner knowing would never face these challenges of not knowing themselves or their desires. When children are in touch with their inner knowing voice, they will be in touch with their needs and know how to meet these needs. They will automatically know that problems arise to be solved, and they will know how to solve them. They will know about their own gifts and know these gifts are meant to be used to make themselves prosperous, happy, healthy, and successful.

Abraham Maslow, a psychologist who studied self-actualizing people (those who actualize all the inherent possibilities of good within themselves), talked about one's inherent gifts or creativity in the following manner in the book, The World of Psychology[*]: "It (creativity) seems to be more a fundamental characteristic of common human nature—a potentiality given to all human beings at birth. Most

---

[*] **Samuel E. Wood, Ellen Green Wood, Denise Boyd,** *The World of Psychology 7th edition* **(Pearson Publishing, Cambridge UK, 2010) page 546**

individuals seem either to retain this fresh and naïve direct way of looking at life, or if they have lost it, as most people do, they later in life recover it."

I believe that the individuals Maslow studied were in touch with their inner knowing and retained an awareness of their goodness. If even a small percentage of people in our world were encouraged to listen to the inner knowing, these people would, by example, teach others. And, perhaps our world and its people would learn to live in harmony. Perhaps if more people were connected to their own inner knowing, they would realize that if we cannot create prosperity for everyone, then it cannot truly exist for anyone.

This may seem like a far-off vision, but it begins with you and your child being willing to know and accept your own innate goodness.

My son said it beautifully to me when he was only five years old. We were talking about hearts and how they represent love. He had a question about a problem with a neighborhood friend. I asked him what his inner knowing voice was telling him to do, and he said he was drawing some hearts to remind himself. I reflected this back in a questioning manner, and he told me, "Mommy, my inner knowing is in my heart." I was touched because I hadn't used this concept with him in such a direct manner before. As we validate the inner knowing voice, the wisdom within grows and grows. This wisdom is what will guide people to know who they are and enable them to succeed in life in ways which most people would never even dream.

Chapter 5

Teaching Right and Wrong

I was washing the dishes when my son asked me, "Mommy, did you hear me?"

"No," I said. "What did you say?"

"I was just talking to myself," he said.

I took that opportunity to validate his inner knowing voice. "Your self is very important to talk to," I said. "There's only one person who will always be with you, and that person is you. Your inner knowing will always tell you what to do and what is right and wrong."

When I asked him if he understood, he replied, "Yes, today my friend told me that I didn't need to ask you before I got on my bike and rode to his house." My son continued by saying, "I was in a hurry and started to leave, and then I heard my inner knowing telling me to come and ask you. I asked and you gave me permission, and I was glad I listened to myself and not what my friend told me to do."

One of the most frustrating situations a parent faces is repeatedly telling their child not to do something and the child continues to do it—even in front of the parent. The parent often reacts by saying, "Why are you still doing that? How many times do I have to tell you? Now, stop it!"

The problem here is misunderstanding. At some level, the child may know he or she is not supposed to act a certain way. However, at a more *unconscious* level, the child persists in the behavior because it *seems* like the right thing for him or her to do at the time based on what he or she thinks will bring the most parental attention—even if it is scolding or punishment. Or the child may need to test the parent to see if he or she will follow through with the promised consequence.

We've all heard the importance of consistency and the need to follow through when we set up limits and consequences. Further, as we do make a 100 percent effort to mean what we say and say what we mean, trust is established.

It is essential that the parent is trustworthy. This is the only way the parent can empower the child to learn to listen to his or her inner knowing. If a child learns to trust the parent, it is easier for the child to learn to trust himself. For example, my son "forgot" to ask before he went to a friend's house. I set up a natural consequence of needing to play at home the next day. As I stick to the consequence, he gets an internal awareness that life is predictable and orderly. He learns about cause and effect and that what he does impacts his world. If I "forget" the consequence, he learns that the world is unpredictable and it is more important to pay attention to external happenings because the lack of order makes him feel crazy. This internal feeling of craziness is not pleasurable. To avoid this pain, he learns to focus on what is going on outside of him for two reasons: first, because of the uncomfortable feelings that come up when his life is unpredictable, and second when a child's life seems random or chaotic, he learns to focus on the outer to try and control the events to bring about order. However, the belief that a child can control outer events is always an illusion, and this illusion of control sets the child up for some very unhealthy behaviors

Let us return to the premise that every child is innately good to understand what I am saying here. Behind every behavior is a belief. This belief at its most basic level has to do with what the child thinks about him or herself and whether the child believes he or she is good or bad. If children have been taught that they are bad, then this belief will color all their actions. They will either act out in a negative way to show the adults what they have taught them is true or go to the opposite extreme and try to prove they are not bad.

Either way, the child's belief about him or herself and the resulting behavior is linked to something or someone that is external. For example, I knew a family whose fifth-born child was their first son. By the time this little boy was born, the father had committed a crime to land him in prison for four years. The mother was obviously overwhelmed and was unable to give the boy the attention he deserved. Because he was a high-needs baby, he cried a lot. The mother, her friends, and relatives began saying, "He acts just like his father, always demanding attention." It is important to note that children are supposed to get attention. The drive to get attended to ensures their survival so that their needs will be met.

The mother began saying to him at a very young age, "You're just like your father, wild and out of control."

The child heard this so frequently that by the time he could walk, he was wild and out of control. His mother was unable to meet his needs in any predictable sense, and he learned that the only way he could get attention was to demand it in a wild and out-of-control manner.

The belief that he was wild and out of control was programmed into him. His true nature was never really validated, and thus, he matched himself to what he heard others saying about him and to him. The inner knowing was drowned out by the beliefs of those adults around him. His own unique nature was ignored. The inner knowing was not validated, and he learned to listen to the voices of everyone external to himself.

To think about this self-fulfilling prophecy in another way, imagine the beliefs that Olympic athletes must have about themselves. They must compete against hundreds of other athletes to make it to the Olympics. What is it that enables them to succeed when others fail? Is it truly because they are indeed better at the particular sport they are excelling in? The individuals in the Olympics must believe that they have the ability to make it or they would never be able to. Finally, think about something you may be trying to master or have mastered in the past. It would not have been possible to master it if you did not believe you could. When you learned to drive a car, you had to believe you could learn or you would not have learned.

When children believe that they are good, they will have the freedom to express themselves in ways that they are guided to from within themselves. Their behavior will be more inner-directed than outer-directed. However, just because a child's basic belief about him or herself is positive does not mean that this child won't test limits and act out. In fact, when children know it is safe to express their curiosity, their behavior may often seem less than desirable. It is important to remember that it is normal and healthy for children to test limits and boundaries at every stage of development. When children believe and know they are basically good, their behavior will be appropriate for their age.

One of the fundamental responsibilities of parents and others who work with children is to teach them the differences between right and wrong. When parents validate the inner knowing in their children while explaining what is right and wrong, the children quickly learn. Then, as they do the right thing, they feel an inner sense of goodness. They also learn that when they intentionally do the wrong thing, they don't experience that same feeling of rightness.

For example, let's say a three-year-old child is feeling overwhelmed with a sense of loss, fear, and anger when her parents bring home their newborn. The little girl is so frustrated about all the demands this infant is making of "her" mommy that when the parents aren't looking, she covers the baby with several blankets, hoping it will just go away or even die. When the parents discover this, the best way to handle this so as to validate the child's knowing and to teach right and wrong is to first try and understand what the child is feeling.

The scenario might go like this when the parents hear the baby crying and see that their three-year-old has covered their baby.

Mom: "Cindy, the baby is crying and I can see that you covered her with several blankets so she is uncomfortable. I wonder if you are feeling angry at the baby."
Cindy: "You like her more than me. I wish you had never brought her home."
Mom: "You know, Cindy, I can understand why you're feeling so angry. I haven't had much time to spend with you, and neither has Daddy."
Cindy: "I hate her! I wish she was dead!"

Note: Young children do not truly understand the concept of death, so when they talk about it, it is essential that the parent remain calm and try to discover what the child's feelings really are when they talk about it. Frequently, a parent will react to the child as if the child had an adult understanding about death—which is not the case at all. This overreaction leads the child to believe that the subject of death and dying is not a safe subject to bring up.

Mom: "You are feeling so angry that you wish the baby would just disappear."
Cindy: "Yeah, you never have time to hold me anymore."
Mom: "You're so sad that I haven't taken to time to hold you like I do the baby."

Cindy: Breaks down and cries uncontrollably.

Mom (Picks Cindy up.): "You are my baby, too. I love you so much. I understand what you are feeling."

Cindy: "Mommy, did I hurt the baby?"

Mom: "No, not really, although you did make her uncomfortable. How did you feel while you were covering her up?"

Cindy: "Not good."

Mom: "I understand that you are angry and sad. Those feelings are real. I will teach you a way to get those feelings out."

Cindy: "Like when you taught me to kick a paper bag until I felt better."

Mom: "Yes, that's right. Good listening to your inner knowing. It's important that you not hurt the baby, and I promise to make time every day just for you."

Cindy: "Mommy, can I hold the baby while you hold me?"

Mom: "Cindy, that's a beautiful idea."

As their inner knowing voice is validated, children learn that doing the right thing brings more good feelings, so they begin to seek that experience and avoid those things that do not foster this inner integrity.

If children haven't experienced this awareness of right and wrong at a deep level of their being, they must learn it through trial and error. They may have to go through many trials that wind up causing numerous problems before they can understand the value of doing the right thing. Certainly, there is joy in doing the right thing and seeing how it makes others feel good, but that is secondary. The primary benefit is the inner reward they receive when their goodness is stimulated.

Ultimately, the easiest way to teach children why they should do right rather than wrong is because doing right makes them feel good. Once, when my son made an unwise choice, I asked him if he had listened to his inner knowing voice. He told me that his inner knowing voice was asleep. When I asked him how he felt about the problem that resulted from his choice, he said, "Mommy, I don't like the way I feel. I feels icky."

In our roles as parents, teachers, and caregivers, we are raising precious children with the potential of being great leaders who can guide our world into a new way of being—if we can just give them the gift of knowing they are good. Thus, it is good and pleasurable to seek this natural state of being and will only have positive consequences across the board.

The choice is ours to make. Do we teach our children they are good and that it is good to seek this inner wholeness? Or do we teach them that who or what they are is not good and that they must look to people and things external to themselves for any experience of the peace of goodness? When children learn this, they have learned to be codependent. My definition of codependency is this: not having an identity except in relationship to other people, places, substances, and activities. As chaotic and random as the world may seem at times, it is much safer to be inner directed.

Chapter 6

Are You Listening Too?

As parents listen to their inner knowing, they are tuning into a place where they are one with their child on a deep and ineffable level. At this level, they know their child in an intuitive way. When parents tune into their inner knowing, they are more clearly able to know what their children need, and they will know how to provide it. There are so many parenting books, and this is good. Yet the advice, concepts, and techniques presented often seem to be in conflict with each other. Parents are the best experts on their children, and as parents avail themselves of all that is available, they can pick and choose that which fits with their own knowing about themselves and their children.

For example, a young child was having chronic headaches. The mother was told by his pediatrician that a certain medication would ease the pain and not to worry about it. Her family physician suggested that she bring her son in for a whole series of allergy tests. Her in-laws "knew" that he wasn't getting enough meat to eat. Somehow, she "knew" that there was something going on that had nothing to do with any of these suggestions. She began charting his headaches and found that they seemed to correlate with the consumption of sugar. As soon as she reduced his sugar intake, the headaches stopped. This is a perfect example of tuning into a deeper level of knowing despite several other louder voices attempting to tell one how it definitely is!

The beauty of a parent's willingness to listen, to really listen to his or her own inner knowing as well as to the child's, is that the parent does not have to be the only one teaching; the child is free to teach the parent as well. An example of this occurred when my son was four years old and we were caught in the grips of a very busy day. My son was not going with the flow or rather, not going with my mighty current of "busy-ness," and I was feeling quite frustrated. He was too, and he was acting it out. What else could he do? I was not taking the time to listen to him or me. Finally, I remembered—I could take a minute and listen to myself and to my son to see what was wrong.

It took all the emotional strength I had to say to him, "Let's stop for a moment and see what's going on." I then said to him, "You really seem upset today."

He replied, "Yes, Mommy, I tried to tell you earlier. I am very frustrated that we had to leave the house so early today so the carpets could be cleaned and I didn't even get a chance to see *Sesame Street* or *Barney*."

My first thought was to react and explain why we needed to leave. Luckily, I listened first and then responded to him instead. I said, "Wow, I can see why you're so frustrated. I would be too. Today is the day you always watch your favorite PBS shows, and we left so early you couldn't even see one."

"Yes, and I'm hungry too. Can we stop and eat lunch now?"

Because I listened and my son responded truthfully, I knew what was more important. My errands could always be done. My relationship with my son and our well-being was so important that we needed to stop and rest for a while. We did, and all our errands got done—and on time!

What is so amazing about this story is that my son, four years old at the time, was able to tell me exactly what was wrong when I stopped to listen to him. He could clearly articulate his problem, and he felt free to tell me because he knew I was listening. Prior to my awareness to stop and listen, he knew I wasn't listening, so he just acted out his frustration. Once I listened to myself and to him, we had a beautiful day. Because I have taught my son the value of listening, he was able to teach me or remind me. I couldn't ask for more—a relationship where my son understands so well what I have taught him that he reminds me when I forget.

As I have been teaching my son about his inner knowing, I have had a remarkable emotional healing. I have become aware at a very deep level that I am also good, and I have access to this inner knowing. Certainly, I knew this in my head before

I could teach it to my son, and yet, this truth was not ingrained in the fabric of my being in such a way that it would be my first impulse, that of turning within to listen to my inner knowing. The first step begins with willingness, and then each person will find his or her own way.

When I am tuned into my inner knowing and I am with another who is also willing to tune within, we come together in a way that is impossible when our focus is outer-oriented. When this occurs with my son, he experiences trust, serenity, and unconditional love. I can't imagine what better gifts I could give him or myself.

Chapter 7

Discipline from the Heart

When my son was in preschool, he befriended a child who was always "causing trouble." Many days, my son would come home with yet another story about how his friend—only four years old—created chaos in the classroom. One day, however, my son didn't have a story about chaos; his story told of a tragic scenario. When his friend had left school early that day, he looked out the window to wave good-bye, and what he saw shocked him. He told me he saw his little friend being struck repeatedly by his mother right out in the parking lot. It seems the child had broken some toys in school that day. When the teacher told the parent about it, my son said, "My friend started to cry, and he ran out of the classroom and jumped into their car. Then his mommy ran as fast as possible and pulled him from the car." My son added, "My friend broke the toys because he was hungry." I asked what he meant, and he said, "Well, my friend came in and asked if I had any snack bars to share because he didn't have breakfast. I told him I didn't, and he started to cry. Then another little girl grabbed the blocks he was playing with, and he stood up and jumped on the dollhouse furniture."

One of the hardest decisions parents must make is how to discipline their children, including whether to hit or spank them. If parents believe in the innate goodness of their children, they could never hit them. When children are struck by someone who supposedly loves them, they not only get the message that they are bad but also that the person hitting them is bad. Think about a stranger hitting your child. Imagine seeing the difference in size and power. Would you think that the person hurting your child was good or bad? The same feelings are there when the person hitting them is someone they know. However, the child often, if not always, internalizes the bad feelings and believes that he or she is bad or his or her primary caregiver wouldn't give this awful pain to him or her.

Spanking does not teach children that they are important or valuable. It has been shown to stop undesirable behavior at times, but it does not give children anything that will enable them to grow into effective, competent adults with high self-esteem and self-worth. Rather, it changes children's self-esteem and teaches them that what is innate is not good.

Spanking does, however, teach a child how to exert arbitrary power and control over others. It teaches the child that the one with the "biggest gun" gets to exert the greatest power. Thus, it creates a relationship of fear rather than love between the parent and child. It teaches children that another person, considerably larger, can come into their space, invade their boundaries and inflict pain. It tells them that they do not have personal boundaries and the person they are *dependent* upon can invade their boundaries whenever they want to.

It is a universal truth that children imitate their parents. They learn best through imitation, modeling, and copying. So when parents demonstrate an attitude of listening, children learn that this is valuable, and they will imitate it. If parents demonstrate that the way to deal with frustration is to strike out at those who are smaller and weaker, the child will learn that this is valuable and copy that behavior. It is your choice—and your responsibility. It is that simple: Children do and say what they observe their parents doing and saying. And yet, if one has used the ineffective method of hitting in an attempt to discipline a child, it may not be easy to get beyond believing that hitting is okay. Hitting has been used for so long—generation after generation—that to stop using it as a disciplinary measure will take a willingness to open our minds and hearts and let new information in.

Barbara Coloroso writes in her book, *kids are worth it! Giving Your Child the Gift of Inner Discipline:*

> ***"Discipline is not judgmental, arbitrary, confusing or coercive. Going back to the Latin roots, to discipline with authority means to give life to learning. Our goal as parents is to give***

life to our child's learning—to instruct, to teach, to help them develop self-discipline—an ordering of the self from the inside, not imposition from the outside. Any technique that does not give life to a child's learning and leaves a child's dignity intact cannot be called discipline—it is punishment, no matter what language it is clothed in. The following four steps of discipline give life to a child's learning in a way that punishment cannot".

Discipline

1. **Shows kids what they have done.**
2. **Gives them ownership of the problem.**
3. **Gives them options of solving the problem.**
4. **Leaves their dignity intact**

Coloroso's four steps validate the child's inner knowing voice. It lets the child know that the parent trusts, respects, and loves the child. When a parent disciplines according to these four steps, the parent must also be listening to her inner knowing.

It is important to address the issue of discipline and punishment because one cannot implement the ideas presented in this book and continue to hit one's children. They are mutually exclusive concepts.

If you have been hitting your children to discipline them and you would like to stop, I encourage you to do three things. First, if you are co-parenting, you must agree with the other parent that you no longer see physical punishment as an effective or appropriate way to discipline.

Second, you need support in finding other ways to discipline. Find two or three parenting books on discipline, and allow yourself to develop strategies that would work for you and your family. As you read these books, remember that everything

---

Barbara Coloroso, *kids are worth it! Giving Your Child the Gift of Inner Discipline,* **Revised edition (Harper Collins, New York, NY, 2002) page 78-79**

you read will not be right for you and your family. Listen to your inner knowing, and devise a system based on what you feel in your heart is best. Third, have a family meeting and discuss with your children your new ideas and plan. And don't forget to get input from your children. Tell them the truth, explaining that you now realize that hitting is not a good way to discipline, that you will stop, and that you need their cooperation. Explain that you have been doing the best you can based on what you learned, but now you have learned a better way to discipline that will help both of you. As you admit your mistake, you are demonstrating to your child that you are not infallible and that you can and do forgive yourself.

Stanley Turecki's book *Emotional Problems of Normal Children,* is an excellent resource for setting up a family meeting. Though there may be times of stress as you make this change in your parenting, you will be giving your children a gift of untold value. You will begin teaching them that they have boundaries. You will demonstrate that it is okay to make mistakes, and it is okay to forgive yourself when do. You will also be restoring their sense of innate goodness so that they can grow up and join the increasing number of people who know they are good and do their best to establish good in the world.

Chapter 8

Healing a Good World

At the age of three, my son had a six-year-old friend who was very interested in Michael Jackson's music. My son went from Raffi and Kermit the Frog to Michael Jackson overnight. He was particularly interested in Jackson's song "Heal the World," and we played it over and over while in the car. During our walks, he would ask me what was wrong with the world and what we needed to do to heal it. I would explain that, in many places around the world, people did not listen to their inner knowing and they were fighting instead of talking. I also told him about children in many, many countries, including our own, who did not have enough food to eat or adequate medical care to help them stay healthy.

Then one day when we were taking a walk downtown, a man approached us and asked for spare change so he could buy a cup of coffee and a sandwich. My son immediately reached into his pocket and gave the man a quarter he had brought from home, and I gave the man a dollar. As we walked away, my son said, "Mommy, were we helping to heal the world?" I told him yes, in a very small way we were, and that the world will be healed when everyone takes small steps towards a solution. Since that incident, every time he sees trash on the ground, he picks it up and tells me he is taking his steps to heal the world.

I find this noteworthy because my son has a view of the world that many other children do not have. He believes in his innate goodness. Because of his belief, he also knows that the world is good and that it just needs some healing. With all the negative things children see going on in the world, it is quite easy for them to develop an attitude that the world is a terrible and scary place to live. This is particularly true of children who believe they are bad.

On the other hand, if a child knows he is good, this sense of goodness is projected into the world. And as a result the child will be empowered to take the steps that only he can take to help solve the world's problems. It is amazing how many miraculous changes have occurred because just one person believed in the good inherent in any given situation. For example, the work that Mother Teresa has done has not only had a healing effect on the world, but she has also inspired thousands of people to do likewise.

I was talking with a man the other day who directs a mentoring program for low-income children. The program encourages children to keep their grades up, and the ones with the right grades are offered a scholarship. The program has become quite successful. Children who had previously shown no interest are now coming to school, doing the work, and achieving high grades. One girl in particular was feeling that this school helped her turn her life around because of the interest that someone had shown in her. She was from a very large family, and being the oldest daughter, she had virtually lost out on her childhood. Her life had been spent helping her single parent mother take care of her younger siblings. She had learned to completely disregard her own needs in order to help her overwhelmed mother survive and meet only the most basic of needs of the family.

When children's needs are not met, they automatically believe something is wrong with them. They believe they are bad. The erroneous belief that one is bad, however, causes severe pain. There is probably no worse pain than to believe that one is truly bad. In order to deal with this type of inner pain, one needs to abandon oneself and create false roles. The false roles keep one separated from one's true self.

Some of these false roles that develop in children (childhood lasting from birth to age eighteen) are rebel, perfectionist, overachiever, beautiful child, outstanding athlete, nerd, drug addict, alcoholic, shopper, good looking, sex addict. Certainly not all these roles are problems in and of themselves, but when played out compulsively in order to hide one's inner pain, these roles become dangerous behaviors that can eventually lead to death.

When children have had to abandon themselves, they are disconnected from their inner knowing. The innate belief that would naturally flow from one's inner knowing that one is inherently good is covered over with the erroneous belief that one is truly inferior and this inferiority must be hidden at all costs.

As we return to the example of the young high school girl in the mentoring program, she had grown up hearing the false belief that who she was at the core was bad. Her false role became that of drug addict/rebel at school. Though she continued to help out at home, she never got her own needs met beyond food, shelter, and meager clothing. However, her school counselor knew she was extremely bright and sensitive. When she was first told about the mentoring program, she laughed. However, when she realized the offer was serious, she cried. She had waited her entire life for someone to see through her roles and negative behavior and see the real gem that she was.

Despite the negative beliefs one may hold about oneself, the truth can never be erased. So she was willing, and even beyond willingness, she was eager to finally put her energy into something that was for her. On the day that she graduated from high school, her entire extended family, numbering over fifty, was there. They all believed in her. The belief that the world was a rough and rotten place had been transformed if only for a while. The girl's belief that she was, in fact, good, was shining so brightly that all of her family members felt that as well.

You may not have been taught that you are basically good. Although the restoration of your belief in yourself may be a painful journey, it is a journey that will bring you infinite possibilities of good. It is a journey well worth the pain, trial, and tribulation. If your parents were not able to teach you this truth about yourself, it is only because they did not know about it themselves; we teach what we know.

It does no good to blame your parents for not teaching something they were incapable of teaching. They may have been the messengers of a dysfunctional system's message, but they did not author the message. The point of this book is not to lay blame at the feet of the messengers. Rather, it is to change the message, and we can change the message. The primary requirement is to be willing to believe in the inherent goodness of oneself and that of all other people. I have heard many people say that they would like to believe in innate goodness but choose not to just in case they are wrong and they are really bad. In doing so, they choose to live their lives in fear. They live their lives based on "what if" rather than listening to the inner knowing and hearing the truth about "what is."

If anyone is having trouble believing in their innate goodness, I ask you to consider how you feel when you look at the breathtaking beauty of a newborn infant. For most, at least, it is impossible to not see innate goodness. Anyone who does not see it is closing off their inner vision, and most likely they are holding an erroneous belief that they are in fact bad.

The journey involves a willingness to reconnect with one's inner child, a common term to indicate the part of us we had to abandon in order to survive. Another term for inner child is "emotional truth." This reconnection can be quite painful. It is a process and does not happen overnight. One needs to be willing to feel the feelings of pain, anger, sadness, and fear that were present when one disconnected from one's true self. Again, this abandonment occurs when one erroneously believes one is innately bad. This belief is impossible to live with, so the disconnection occurs and the birth of false selves or false roles begins.

This journey home has been described in so many beautiful and clear ways. Alan Alda captures the essence of the journey in the following poem:

> ***Be brave enough to live life creatively. The creative is the place where no one else has ever been. You have to leave the city of your comfort and go into the wilderness of your intuition. You can't get there by bus, only by hard work and risk and by not quite knowing what you're doing. What you'll discover will be wonderful. What you'll discover will be yourself. –Alan Alda-***

I am sure you have had your own awakenings—crystal clear moments or flashes of light that tell you that the erroneous beliefs you hold about yourself are wrong. In these holy moments, one feels hope that the negative beliefs are false.

One notices the weight of carrying these beliefs and may be motivated to take some action. Further, many people are highly motivated to change these beliefs because if they do not, they know that these negative beliefs will be passed on to their children. The greatest gift that you can ever give your child or the children of the world is your own wholeness. Even if children have grown up watching their parents abandon themselves and then medicate the pain, the inner healing that occurs in children of any age when they see their parents connecting to their own truth is beyond measurement. When individuals see their parent choose the inner journey home, they are then called to do likewise. And just as the parents most likely taught the children to abandon themselves in a way that no one else but parents can teach, the parent can re-teach the child and guide them to their own selves. So I challenge you to continue on the journey to your own wholeness. You *will* stimulate the inner knowing in others when you listen to and speak from yours.

Chapter 9

Trust: The Gift of Teaching Yourself and Your Child to Listen to Their Inner Knowing

It is January 7, 2015, and I have been working on this book for twenty-four years. The best part about working on it for so long is that I have been practicing the ideas in this book, not only with my son, but I have been doing my best to make it a daily practice to connect with and listen to my inner knowing. This commitment has brought me to a deep level of growth and awareness. Though the practice of listening deeply within and then doing one's best to act from this deep awareness does not prevent challenges, it enables one to move through the challenges in a heroic way. I say heroic because a true hero takes the highest and best action, based on his or her own internal sense of what is right. I believe the only way to bring peace to our world is by being willing to listen to one's inner knowing, set good boundaries, speak one's truth from the "I" and then be willing to listen in this way to those around us. This process begins by bringing peace to our own hearts, then to our own personal relationships with family and friends. Through the last twenty-four years, my family and I have gone through many challenges, as do most people. My husband and I each lost a sister at their age of forty-five. We have gone through many job changes that caused huge stress for our entire family, have moved three times, and have faced and survived many other crisis-type issues.

Because we chose to face them by listening first to our inner knowing, we wound up stronger and more happy than had we not gone through them by listening to our own inner knowing and then to one another's as well.

I titled this last chapter "Trust" because a major gift that comes from listening to one's inner knowing is that we learn to trust ourselves. The only way to trust in any relationship is to first trust oneself in such a way that we know we will never betray ourselves in thought, word, or deed. This is not an easy task, but again, it is the only way to be able to trust others. This kind of trust is based on true integrity. That is, no matter what another says or does, we will always listen to ourselves first before we respond and respond according to our own inner knowing. An example of this type of trust can be seen in the following story (names and outer details changed):

I had a female client, aged eighteen, who was in a violent relationship with her boyfriend. He was being emotionally and verbally abusive to her, and she was quite afraid of him. She came to see me about how to get him to stop doing this to her as she feared that the verbal abuse could lead to physical abuse.

I learned that what her boyfriend was doing was similar to the way her mother treated her. As a child, she had learned to ignore this fear and do her best to placate her mother when her mother would scream and call her names. She actually had no other choice as a child at home. However, now that she no longer lived at home, I helped her see that she did have a choice.

In therapy, I helped her connect with her own feelings of fear but also helped her connect with her own sense of power. Through this process, she did connect to her inner knowing and realized that this relationship was abusive and was not serving her. She was able to end the relationship, and in doing this, she connected to her own sense of worthiness.

This example shows that by listening within, we reconnect to our own sense of self-esteem. I say our "own sense of self-esteem" because most people's self-esteem is based on what others think, say, and do around them rather than a deep inner awareness that who they are is enough and is worthy, just because they are.

In my personal journey of listening to my own inner knowing, I have learned through experience, through study, and through trial and error that we are all "equal to." Most people act like they are either better than or less than those around them. When people act as if they are better than those around them, they are going into entitlement and grandiosity. When people act as if they are less than those around them, they are going into shame or a sense that there is something wrong with them. The truth is, most humans, if not all, go into grandiosity and shame on a daily basis. The only antidote to this is to be willing to understand that we are all "equal to", and the only way to truly practice this is to listen to one's own inner knowing.

As we practice the fact that we are all "equal to" by listening within, and then communicating and acting from this level of awareness, we are learning to trust ourselves in such a way that we know we will not betray ourselves. From this deep awareness of trusting ourselves, we can then learn to trust others because we trust ourselves first.

A great example of learning to trust myself comes from being a horse-guardian or horse-parent the last seven years. (I say guardian here because I do not own my horse as much as I am her guardian or parent.)

When I first got my horse to do equine-assisted psychotherapy, I was literally inundated with information from every other horse guardian I met. And everyone seemed to have different opinions on every aspect of horse care. There was no limit to the differing information that was given to me on horse care, such as diet, shoeing, blanketing, riding, wound care, etc.

Initially, I found myself quite disoriented trying to make sense of all the opinions that were being offered to me. Then one day, I realized that if I were to ever be the best caretaker of my wonderful horse, I needed to listen gratefully to others, but in the end, I needed to listen to my own inner knowing and to begin to trust that I would do the best thing for my horse, even if it was not what the countless other people were telling me.

And in my willingness to listen to my own inner knowing about Harmony's care, I have come to understand that horses seem to live from this place of inner knowing or it might better be called instinct in the horse.

I have watched Harmony and her herd of twenty-five horses live outside for seven years. They get to live in a natural habitat, roaming over three hundred acres. Most of the horses are not shod, and most do not go into a stall at night. They instinctively know how to live outside. They do have plenty of hay and fresh water in the winter, and in the summer, they delight in a sumptuous pasture of the greenest and sweetest grass and wildflowers that I have encountered in Colorado. They do have leaders, those in the mid-range, and those at the bottom of the so-called totem pole. The ones at the top of the pecking order tend to guide the herd as far as when to go get water, when to move to their natural shelter under the trees, and when to be cautious. It seems that when a new horse comes into the herd, the leaders sometimes make the horse wait on the outside of the herd until the leader horses know this horse is safe. Of course all of this is my perception based on connecting with my inner knowing and my feelings and thoughts, etc. Another person would have a different take perhaps.

The point is that as I have watched the horses live together in safety and mostly in harmony, I wistfully hope that someday humans will learn how to have such a healthy community. (Please see the last pages of this book for a story about Harmony and her herd and how we communicate from the heart)

For now, as I close this last chapter of this book, I have a sweet challenge for you. First of all, can you imagine how the life of you and your children (no matter how old they are) would change if *you* first learned to listen to your inner knowing and if you began respecting their inner knowing?

Everything would change: If your child wanted to go to college to become a policeman, you would process this choice with him or her even if you did not agree.

If your child wanted to become a musician, you would support your child in this endeavor, and if you disagreed, you would ask if he or she minded hearing of some other ideas. If he or she said no, then you would respect that, knowing your child has the same inner knowing as you do.

If you realized that you had a dream of singing that was stuffed into the shadow of your consciousness, you would pull that dream out of your shadow and take one tiny step toward the fulfillment of this.

If you had a desire to say, for example, get a horse, and even if you had absolutely no idea how you would pay for this horse or where you would board it or even how you could learn to take care of it, you, again, would take one tiny step toward the fulfillment. (This story about the horse is my true story!)

You see, our world is recreated every time a person decides to identify his or her dream and believe that it is possible. And we do this by simply taking the next step. Again, all we ever need to do to make a dream come true is simply be willing to take the first tiny step. When we take that step, we can then see the next step and so on and so forth.

The reason I am a mother is that I listened to my inner knowing about a deep desire and dream to be a mother. Though I said "no way" to this dream for many years, one day, I finally realized after a deep meditation, that if nothing were standing in my way, I would have a boy named Christopher. Well that dream came true, as you know, and since that wondrous dream, my dreams keep coming true one step at a time.

Are you willing to begin to heal our world in the only way you can, by making your dreams come true? Then it is time to listen to your inner knowing. It will never, ever fail you.

And that is my promise to you.

For more about these concepts, please visit my website to see when a workshop is coming to your neck of the woods. www.UnityWholenesscenter.com

To book Suzanne for a speaking engagement, workshop or retreat, you may reach her directly at: equinelites@aol.com

With Infinite Gratitude to the following people for the ways you were present to me, either professionally, personally or both. Your amazing and authentic presence enabled me to keep my commitment to my authentic path and your support made all the difference.

Dianne Veno, Jan Santora, Sarah Griffin, Bernardo Monserrat PhD, Roger Ware PhD, Father Ted at Assumption Abbey in Ava, MO, Ted Klontz, PhD,, Lynne Thomas of EAGALA.org, Mike Fitch, PhD, Linda McCabe, PhD, Michael Denhof, PhD, Graham Sterritt, PhD, Kristi Stucz, Jean Clark, Rosemarie Kelly, Nan Sloane, Dr. Michael Herman, DVM, of Belcaro Animal Hospital in Denver and your amazing and perfect care of our dogs.

* The therapists I was able to work with at Onsite Workshops,,
* High School teachers: Mrs. Bloemker, Mrs. Williams, Mr. Klene
* College Professors, B. B. Morris, PhD, Ami Sha'Ked, PhD
* Unity Ministers, Reverends Marvin and Kathryn Anderson, Reverend Janet Manning, Reverend Ed Rabel, Reverend Annie Lonardelli.

~ And to Debbie Wetmore, because of you and your friendship and your generosity with your horses, my life took a new direction that would have never have happened without you.

More Acknowledgements

The following people are amazingly gifted people who have blessed me and the entire planet and they have done it by being themselves. Please look at their contact information to see if their work may bring sustenance to you on your journey, the ONE and ONLY JOURNEY that your soul asks you to take.

Christopher James Addison Cross Carter www.seetocenter.com

I mention Christopher, my son first because were it not for him, I would not have written this book. He is a musician par excellence. He was in his first band in 3rd grade. He has been in bands that he directs ever since. Currently he is in the band, SEE TO CENTER. Here is what the web-site says about Christopher and his band members.

"Based around the catchy songwriting of their front man, Chris Carter, See to Center blends thick organic textures with traditional electronic pop to create a unique musical experience. Formed in the summer of 2014, See to Center's music captures the feelings and atmosphere intrinsic to a summer day's slow fade into the dark of night. Bolstered by a passion for life, Carter's lyrics reflect the harmony and dissonance found in everyday struggles, his acoustic guitar providing waves of shimmering bliss over driving beats. Backing Carter is percussionist John Wiberg and bassist Rob Wiberg. John uses an array of exotic drums and flowing shakers to cultivate a hypnotic rhythm that weaves through the music, elevating each song to greater heights. Rob ties it all together bringing a pounding groove to each song.

Sliding between funky slap riffs and creamy melodies Rob keeps toes tapping and heads bobbing. See to Center are currently writing and recording songs to form into an album"……

JOHN BRADSHAW www.JohnBradshaw.com

Author, TV Personality, Mentor, Innovator, Philosopher, Counselor, Theologian, Educator, and Elder. For the past four decades, John Bradshaw has combined his exceptional skills as the role of counselor, author, management consultant, theologian, philosopher, and public speaker, becoming one of the leading figures in the fields of addiction/recovery, family systems, relationships, Spiritual and emotional growth, and management training. John brought the phrases dysfunctional families and inner child into mainstream society. His dynamic training and therapies are practiced all over the world. A much sought out speaker, John has truly touched and transformed the lives of millions. He was elected by a group of his peers as *'one of the most influential writers on emotional health in the 20th Century.'*

Barbara Coloroso www.kidsareworthit.com

Barbara Coloroso is an internationally recognized speaker and author in the areas of parenting, teaching, school discipline, non-violent conflict resolution and reconciliatory justice. She is an educational consultant for school districts, the medical and business community, the criminal justice system and other educational associations around the world.

Barbara has served as a classroom teacher, a laboratory school instructor, and a university instructor. She is the author of five international bestsellers.

Russell Friedman www.griefrecoverymethod.com

Russell Friedman is Executive Director of The Grief Recovery Institute and co-author with John W. James, of five books: ***The Grief Recovery Handbook, When Children Grieve, Moving On, Moving Beyond Loss,*** and ***The Grief Recovery Handbook for Pet Loss.*** They have also co-authored hundreds of feature articles on "people's reaction to loss and what to do about it." Russell has often been the Grief

Recovery expert on CNN and other new media, appearing after 9/11, and many other major international grief related events that dominated the news. ON the web at www.griefrecoverymethod.com. Email: rfriedman@griefrecoverymethod.com Ph: 800-334-7606 Ext 12 Fax: 818-907-9329

Ted Klontz www.Tedklontz.com

Ted Klontz Ph.D (Psychology) based in Nashville TN., has authored and/or contributed to six books on Behavioral Finance, is a published researcher, professional speaker, trainer, workshop designer and facilitator, mentor, travelling extensively and internationally in his role as consultant and troubleshooter to a major entertainment management group, a private practitioner working with professional athletes, entertainers, and high profile families, corporations, couples, and individuals, as well as the average citizen.

Dr. Klontz is a noted pioneer in the development and application of unique tools and techniques for helping people change their troublesome behaviors. He has served as an advisor to Congressional Committees, the Defense Department, local, national and international radio, TV, and print media.

Dr. Klontz's most recent projects include that of a contributing author to a seventh book on changing financial behaviors in conjunction with Kansas State University, appearances on the OWN network, and creating and conducting interpersonal communication workshops around the world.

Mark Nepo www.Marknepo.com

Mark Nepo moved and inspired readers and seekers all over the world with his #1 *New York Times* bestseller **The Book of Awakening**. Beloved as a poet, teacher, and storyteller, Mark has been called "one of the finest spiritual guides of our time," "a consummate storyteller," and "an eloquent spiritual teacher." His work is widely accessible and used by many and his books have been translated into more than twenty languages. A bestselling author, he has published seventeen books and recorded twelve audio projects. In 2015, he was given a Life-Achievement Award by AgeNation. And in 2016, he was named by *Watkins: Mind Body Spirit* as one of the 100 Most Spiritually Influential Living People.

Terry Real www.Terryreal.com

Terry Real is an internationally recognized Family Therapist, Speaker and author. Terry founded the Relational Life Institute (RLI), offering workshops for couples, individuals and parents around the country along with a professional training program for clinicians wanting to learn his RLT (Relational Life Therapy) methodology. A family therapist and teacher for more than twenty five years, Terry is the best-selling author of *I Don't Want to Talk About It: Overcoming the Secret Legacy of Male Depression* (Scribner, 1997), the straight-talking *How Can I Get Through to You? Reconnecting Men and Women* (Scribner, 2002), and most recently *The New Rules of Marriage: What You Need to Make Love Work* (Random House). Terry knows how to lead couples on a step-by-step journey to greater intimacy — and greater personal fulfillment.

Cindy Wigglesworth www.deepchange.com.

Cindy Wigglesworth is the author of *SQ21: The Twenty-One Skills of Spiritual Intelligence*, a recognized expert in the field of Spiritual Intelligence, and an experienced leadership coach and corporate consultant. Her SQ21 spiritual intelligence self-assessment is a diversity-appropriate and skills-based way of discussing powerful human motivators and success factors. After working for 20 years in a Fortune 50 company in Human Resources she formed her own company in 2000 and created her multiple intelligence approach to leadership developing. Using a combination of four intelligences (physical, mental, emotional and spiritual) she coaches senior executives to overcome barriers to their own career success and helps them lead their organizations to greatness.

Rev Nat Carter

And finally, I acknowledge my husband of 30 years, Nat Carter.
Because of your willingness to support me in mothering our son, Christopher, I was able to have great flexibility as we co-ministered several churches in our capacity as Unity Ministers.

I think you are one of, if not the best, Unity Minister in the country. Your Sunday services are a work of art and Heart. You fulfill the other tasks in ministry with perfection. And, you are a great example of following your inner knowing with regard to making a career dream come true.

Rev. Nat Carter tells us that throughout his professional life, his focus has been to serve and empower others to grow into their divine potential. He has achieved this with teaching positive, practical, mystical spirituality. In his own words, "I have been working with a number of ministries as a transitional ministry specialist for the last few years. My preparation for this and my experience of this has been extraordinarily valuable for me and, I believe, for the ministries served". Rev. Carter has a B.A. in Russian and East Asian Area Studies, a Masters in education and is a graduate of Unity Ministerial Education Program. He has been serving as a Unity Minister since 1985. He was Senior Minister at Unity Church of Denver for a period of ten years and since 2013 has been serving as a transitional ministry specialist for Unity Worldwide Ministries.

You may contact Nat at: Unitynat@yahoo.com

About Suzanne Carter

Suzanne lives near Evergreen, Colorado with her husband, Nat Carter of 30 years, her dog of many lifetimes, her horse, Harmony. She is able to see her Son, Christopher, and his dog frequently as they live near Fort Collins. She is in private practice and does many workshops and speaking engagements on the topics of this book. She is dedicated to your Wholeness and your Happiness. To contact her, visit her website: www.UnityWholenessCenter.com

And the story I promised you about:

~Harmony, my Equine daughter~

I have had my wonderful horse, Harmony for almost 7 years. She is my first and only horse so far and I say with 100% honesty, I am a different person because of my relationship with Harmony. Or actually, I am more of my truest self rather than a different person.

Horses are amazing creatures. They have learned to live safely in their herds for millions of years and they are a prey animal. That is, they are not a predator. They do not seek to kill other animals to eat; they are vegetarians. Being a prey animal especially means that the horse is highly motivated to stay connected to their herd. They know that their greatest protection lies in this connection with their herd; a truth that I wish humans would return to.

Harmony is a thoroughbred, meaning she is one of the grand race horses. She is the great grand-daughter of Secretariat! And as a descendant of Bold Ruler (Secretariats daddy), she has a marking on her right shoulder that descendants of bold ruler often have.

Every year from early November until about late April to mid May, I take Harmony extra food to eat nearly every day beyond the hay and grasses that she gets at her 1000 acre ranch where I board her. She tends to lose weight in the winter and the extra food helps plus I have the most amazing experience with her every single time I see her.

Today, I went to the ranch to take her the extra food. My therapy dog, Jessie the Golden Retriever, and I decided to take a walk first before we fed Jessie's 1000 pound sister. We walked North of where the horses were grazing.......and as we were coming back south toward them, there appeared a large herd of elk. Elk as prey animals are afraid of dogs of course. So, as soon as they saw Jessie and me (also a predator in their eyes), they all looked up and began walking and then running toward Harmony and her herd. The elk got out of our sight just as Harmony and her 24 herd mates saw them running. Horses are not afraid of elk but when they saw the elk running, they decided that there may be something dangerous, so they decided to run..........they circled around and soon were running straight at Jessie and me. Jessie and I stepped out of their immediate path and I was able to simply revel in the site of 25 horses all running as fast as they could toward us and then past us. I saw Harmony as she ran past; she looked at me, almost stopped but then kept her pace in line with her herd.

When the horses got to the top of the hill, I saw them all run to where a large grove of Ponderosa Pines is and they stopped.

I thought I would go get Harmony and bring her back to her extra food. Jessie and I started walking up the hill where the horses had just been running and I saw the very tips of a horse's ears on the horizon. I wondered if it might just be Harmony. My" heart -thought" was right; it was Harmony, my most beautiful and exquisite equine daughter. I said a quiet greeting to her; she kept looking at me but just stood there. So, I followed her non-verbal cue and stopped. We looked at each other for a moment and without a word, I communicated to her that I loved her and that it was o.k. to just go be with her herd. Almost immediately, she walked slowly over to one of her best friends, Sunny, who is a magical horse that makes you feel loved whenever he looks at you.

I knew in my heart that Harmony is now ready for wonderful summer activities and that she does not need me to bring her the extra food anymore until the winter snows come again.

I walked away with a profound peace in my mind and love in my heart. And, we did this all without a spoken word.

Printed in the United States
By Bookmasters